Macmillan/McGraw-Hill
Looking at Earth

Dear Amy

Neumeyer Channel

Grenada

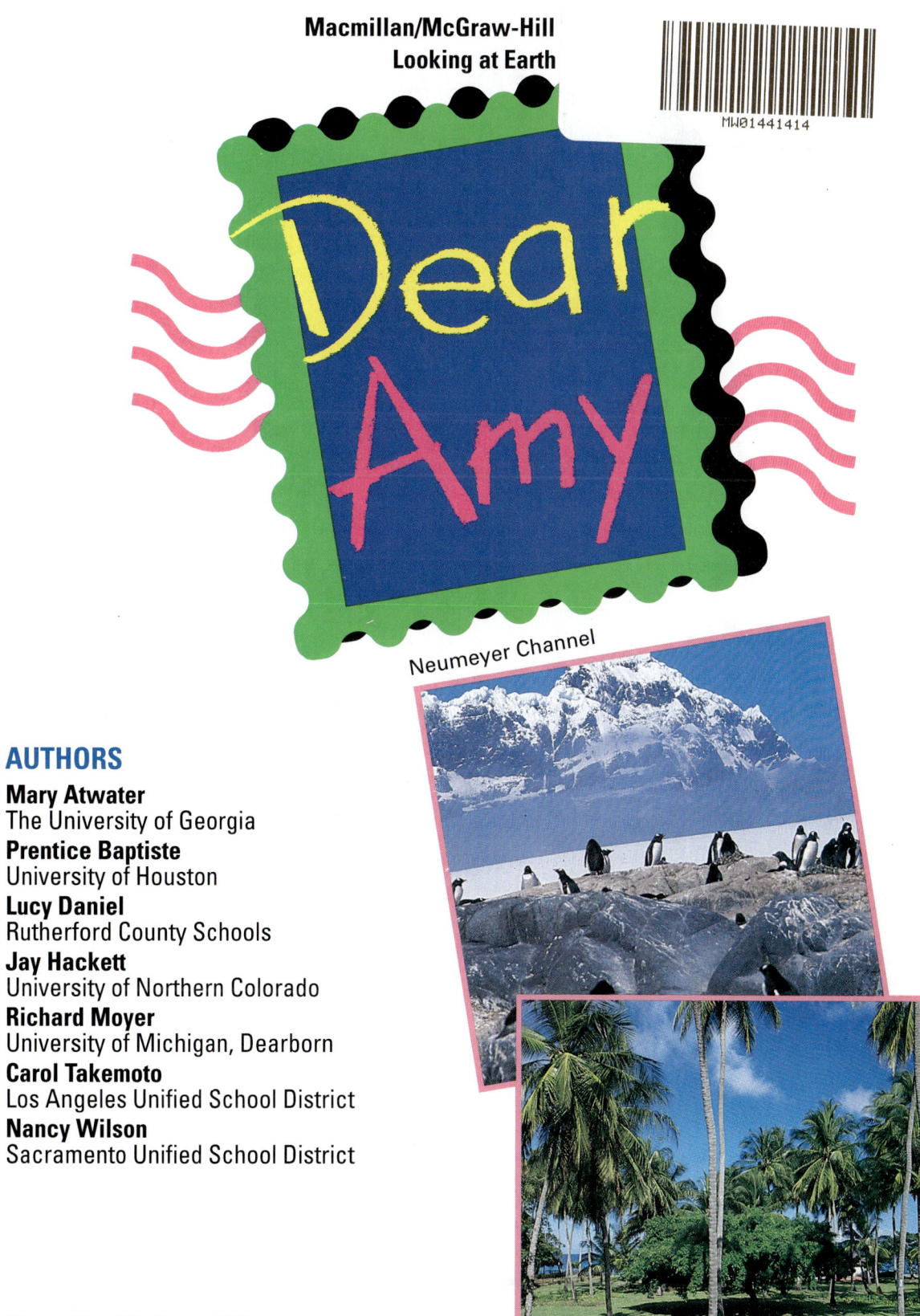

AUTHORS

Mary Atwater
The University of Georgia
Prentice Baptiste
University of Houston
Lucy Daniel
Rutherford County Schools
Jay Hackett
University of Northern Colorado
Richard Moyer
University of Michigan, Dearborn
Carol Takemoto
Los Angeles Unified School District
Nancy Wilson
Sacramento Unified School District

**Macmillan/McGraw-Hill
School Publishing Company**
New York   Chicago   Columbus

Dear Amy

Themes:
Patterns of Change / Systems and Interactions

Lessons
What's the Weather? 3
Does the Weather Make
 a Difference? 18

Activities!

EXPLORE
How Does the Weather Change? 6
Does Weather Matter? 20

TRY THIS
Make a Wind Finder 5
What Can Be Blown? 9
Catch the Rain 13
Hot or Cold 15
What's Special About Seasons? 23
Pick a Card 27

Will It Be Sunny? Will It Rain?
Focus on Technology 29

Theme **T** PATTERNS of CHANGE

What's the Weather?

"Mom! Mom!" Juan shouted. "I got a letter from Amy!" Juan opened the letter. Something blew away. He ran after it.

Juan had to run fast. Finally he caught up with it. It was a picture of Amy. As he picked it up, he noticed leaves blowing all around. "It is really windy today," he thought.

Minds On! How can you tell it is windy?

Try This Activity!

Make a Wind Finder

1. Make a paper loop and tape it together.

2. Tie on a handle made of yarn.

3. Tape on paper strips.

4. Take your wind finder outdoors and observe what happens.

EXPLORE

Activity!

How Does the Weather Change?

Wind is only one part of the weather. Have you ever noticed how weather changes?

What You Need

outdoor thermometer

wind finder

Activity Log

weather chart

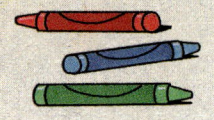

crayons

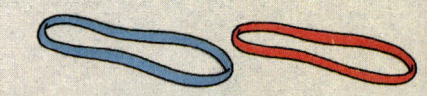

2 colored rubber bands

What To Do

1. Find the temperature each morning and afternoon at the same time for a week. Mark the temperatures. Record on the chart.

6

2. Use the wind finder each morning and afternoon. Record on the chart.

	Monday		Tuesday		Wednesday		Thursday		Friday	
	AM	PM	AM	PM	AM	PM	AM	PM	AM	PM
Temperature	🌡️	🌡️	🌡️	🌡️						
Wind	(yes) no	yes (no)	(yes) no	(yes) no						
Rain 💧💧💧 Clouds ☁️ Sun ☀️ Snow ❄️	☀️	☀️	☀️	☁️💧💧💧						

3. Record if there was rain, snow, clouds, or sunshine.

What Happened?

1. What weather changes did you observe?
2. When did the changes happen?
3. Draw pictures in your **Activity Log** to show what you observed each day.

EXPLORE

Juan walked over to where his mom was gardening. "Why is the wind important?" he asked.

How is this young spider using the wind?

How do people use wind?

TRY THIS Activity!

What Can Be Blown?

1. Use your breath to blow on each object. Which ones could you move?
2. Use a piece of cardboard to fan each object. Which ones moved?

How do plants use wind?

How are these animals using the wind?

9

"What is wind, Mom?" Juan asked.
"You know that air is all around Earth," Juan's mom answered. "Well, wind is moving air. The wind can change from day to day."

"Have you noticed any other changes, Juan?" his mother asked.

"It was warm and now it is getting cold," he answered. "Oh, look at all those clouds! I think it's going to rain."

Rain clouds

Minds On! Can you tell when it is going to rain? How?

Just then Juan felt a raindrop hit his hand. Juan and his mom ran toward the house.

TRY THIS Activity!

Catch the Rain

1. Make a rain catcher by setting a funnel in the top of a plastic bottle.
2. Label 5 bottles with the days of the week.
3. Each day set out a new rain catcher. Take the old one in and save it.
4. At the end of the week, look at all 5 rain catchers. Which has the most rain? Which has the least?

Juan and his mom read the letter from Amy and waited for the rain to stop. Soon the sun came out and Juan ran outside to play. He got too warm and took off his jacket. "I wonder how warm it is now?" he thought.

Minds On! How can Juan find out how warm it is? •

TRY THIS ACTIVITY!

Hot or Cold

1. Go outside with your teacher.
   Choose 3 places you think are warm.
   Put a thermometer in each place.
2. After 10 minutes, check the thermometers. Which place was the warmest?
3. Now do the same thing in 3 places you think are cool. Which place was the coolest?

"The weather changes a lot here. I wonder if the weather everywhere changes a lot?" Juan would ask Amy about her weather.

Dear Amy,
This morning the 🌬️ was blowing 🍃🍃🍃.
The ☀️ was shining.
Mom and I were outside and we saw ☁️.
Then it started to 💧💧💧💧.
Now the ☀️ is shining.
It is warm.
What is the weather like where you live?
                Love,
                Juan

Minds On! Write a letter to Amy. Tell what the weather is like where you live.

Theme T · PATTERNS of CHANGE

Does the Weather Make a Difference?

Juan looked at the picture Amy had sent. "It must be warmer in Australia right now than it is here," he said.

Minds On! Why does Juan think it is warmer where Amy lives?

Do you know that the weather is different in different places around the world?

Some places have many different kinds of weather.

Summer

Winter

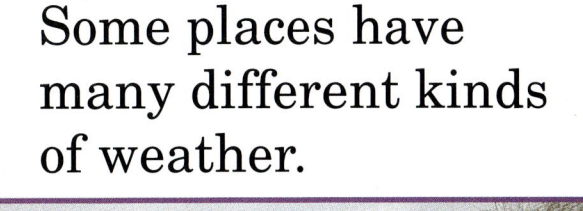

In some places, it is warm most of the time.

In other places, it is cold all the time.

19

EXPLORE

Activity!

Does Weather Matter?

What kinds of choices do you make because of the weather?

What You Need

crayons

Activity Log

objects you use and wear in different weather

What To Do

1. Look at the objects. Tell how each one is used.

20

2. Put all of the things used on warm, sunny days in one group.
3. Put all of the things used on cold days in one group.
4. Put all of the things used on rainy days in one group.

What Happened?

1. Draw a picture in your **Activity Log** to show what you wear and do on warm, sunny days.
2. Draw a picture to show what you wear and do on cold days.
3. Group the objects another way.

EXPLORE

21

"Mom, why is Amy wearing shorts in this picture?" Juan asked. His mom replied, "Well, her letter says it is spring in Australia."

Fall

Winter

22

Minds On! Some places have four seasons each year. They are fall, winter, spring, and summer. What season is it where Juan lives? How can you tell?

Spring

Summer

TRY THIS Activity!

What's Special About Seasons?

1. Fold your paper into four parts.
2. Draw a picture of each season.
3. Draw the seasons in order.
4. Glue the paper to the box.

Which season follows winter?

23

"Could you take a picture of me raking leaves?" Juan asked his mom. "I will send it to Amy. Then she will know it is fall here." Juan's mom nodded and Juan ran toward the door.

"Wait!" called Juan's mom. "It is chilly outside. You need to wear a jacket."

Minds On! Where Juan lives the air gets colder in the fall. He wears a jacket. How do you dress for each season?

After Juan's picture was taken, he finished raking the leaves. He decided to build a house out of leaves.

Juan looked at his leaf house and said, "Maybe I'll build real houses someday. This is good weather for it."

Minds On! Why is weather important to the people in these pictures?

Snowplow operator

Mail carrier

Teacher and student

TRY THIS Activity!

Pick a Card

1. Pick a job card.
2. Spin the weather spinner.
3. Tell how the weather will make a difference in your job.

27

"Can we walk to the post office to mail my letter tomorrow, Mom?" Juan asked. "Watch the news and see what the weather will be," she answered.

Minds On! Why do you think Juan's mom wants to know what the weather will be tomorrow?

Focus on Technology

Will It Be Sunny? Will It Rain?

Many people like to know what the weather will be tomorrow or the next day. Weather satellites in space take pictures of Earth. These pictures help people tell what the weather will be.

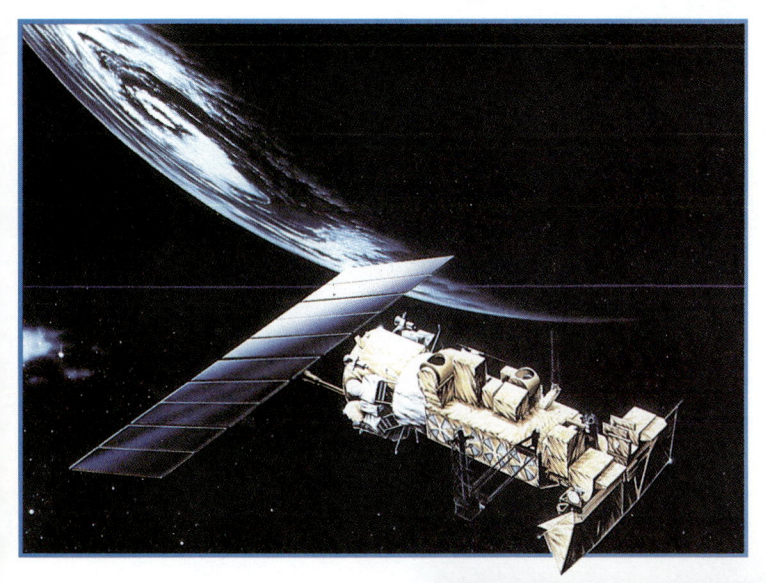

A weather satellite in space

A weather system from space

my Brown
angaroo Street
Manly, New South Wales
Australia 2095

Juan and his mom walked to the post office in the bright sunshine. "I would like to visit Australia someday," Juan said. "I think I would go in December because I love summer."

Listening Vocabulary/Index

air, page 10
Air is all around us.

fall, page 23
Fall is a season.

seasons, page 23
Some places on Earth have four seasons.

spring, page 23
Spring is a season.

summer, page 23
Summer is a season.

weather, page 16
Weather is changes in the air outdoors.

wind, page 10
Wind is moving air.

winter, page 23
Winter is a season.